A Summary of the
BIBLE

JOHN ALFRED

ISBN 978-1-0980-5899-9 (paperback)
ISBN 978-1-0980-5900-2 (digital)

Christian Faith Publishing, Inc.
832 Park Avenue
Meadville, PA 16335
www.christianfaithpublishing.com

Printed in the United States of America

In memory of John M.

Preface

I was raised in a family that did not practice any particular faith. Consequently, I had no understanding of what the Bible was about nor what the Jewish or Christian faith was about. By the time I was in high school, I did not believe that God existed. God was a myth to me.

Between my first and second year of college, I had a powerful experience. It was like an awakening; I realized that God existed. From that time forth, I was seeing with new eyes. I could look at the stars and know God was out there. I also knew there was some kind of spiritual world.

A few months later, I saw a book on my childhood bookshelf that I never read: *The Story of Salvation.* The book turned out to be a summary of the Bible. For the first time in my life, I learned what was in the Bible: how it began with God creating the world, how man was created, and how God has been and will be directing human history to its end. When I finished the book, I understood who the Jewish people were, who Jesus was, why Jesus was crucified, how he rose from the dead, and how the world will eventually end with a final judgment. Christianity made sense. I wanted to be a Christian and by God's irresistible grace eventually became one a couple years later.

Over the last forty years, I have grown in my experience in the Christian faith. Over the last thirty years, I have read the Bible from cover to cover every year. Over the last twenty years, I have studied theology. Given what I have learned from reading the Bible repeatedly and from the teachings of widely respected theologians throughout church history (e.g. St. Augustine, Martin Luther, John Calvin, and Jonathan Edwards), I was comfortable to express the Bible's overall message in the form of this summary.

From my studies, I learned that there are three stages of having a saving faith. The first stage is the informative stage, where the person becomes informed of what the faith is about. The second stage is the agreement stage, where the person agrees that the information is true. The third stage is the trusting stage, where the person trusts and relies on the information as the truth and will stake his/her life on it.

The purpose of this summary is to help with the informative stage. As I needed at the beginning of my Christian experience, this summary is to help the reader understand what is in the Bible from start to finish. Whoever reads this summary should know that having this summary in his or her hands is not a coincidence. It is God who draws us to Himself. My hope and prayer is that God will use this summary to inform readers how they can make peace with God; have all their misdeeds, great and small, be completely forgiven by God; and commit themselves into a loving and intimate relationship with the Father, the Son, and the Holy Spirit. Without a doubt, to make peace and commit to an intimate relationship with God is the *most* important decision anyone could make. Indeed, such a decision is a matter of eternal life or eternal separation.

Another purpose of this summary is to be a resource to those who are saved. Saved Christians realize and embrace their duty to spread the good news to others. They also understand and trust that God will work through their efforts to achieve his eternal purposes.

Without holiness no one will see the Lord
—Hebrews 12:14 ESV, Written in a letter to Christian Hebrews circa 60 A.D

Starting from the first Book of the Bible—Genesis:
 The Bible begins with how the Father, the Son, and the Holy Spirit created the visible universe as we know it and everything within. Out of nothing, something was created by something not of the universe, something self-existent and mutually exclusive from the universe—God. Natural science will not be able to explain the supernatural. Furthermore, it is a scientific (and logical) impossibility for the universe to create itself.

Included in God's creation was his creation of the first man, Adam, and the first woman, Eve. They had physical bodies that were created to exist for eternity; their bodies would not decay nor die. Different from all the other creatures on the earth, Adam and Eve were made in the image of God, having the capacity to relate, think, plan, manage, create, etc.

Our first parents were placed in paradise here on earth (Eden—somewhere in the Middle East), and every day, they lived in the presence of God. Among the fruit-bearing trees, there were two particular trees: the tree of life and the tree of the knowledge of good and evil. Adam and Eve were allowed to eat from any tree; however, God commanded them *not* to eat from the tree of the knowledge of good and evil. Should they disobey God's command, they would experience physical death; their bodies would no longer be eternal. This is known as a *conditional* covenant. Adam and Eve would live forever as long as they kept the one command.

Among God's creation were angels. They are creatures; however, they do not have physical bodies like mankind. They are unseen spiritual beings that continue to exist in our physical world (although they appeared sometimes in the Bible, like to Abraham, Jacob, Joshua, Joseph, and Mary, to name a few times). One of the chief angels, Satan, rebelled against God. To this day, Satan, whose power exceeds any human power on earth, along with a host of other demonic angels, exist in this world but are under God's sovereign rule.

Satan deceived our first parents into thinking that if they ate the fruit from the tree of the knowledge of good and evil, they could be like God. Satan flatly lied to them by saying that they would not die if they ate the forbidden fruit. The idea of being like God became extremely attractive to them, and so they ate. Instantly, they realized their guilt of breaking God's command and became ashamed.

In futility, Adam and Eve tried to hide from God; but God knew exactly where they were and confronted them. Although they tried to pass the blame, our first parents knew that they disobeyed God's command. God pronounced his judgment: from dust they were created, to dust they would return. No longer pure and blameless, i.e. holy, they could no longer live in God's presence. Death and decay would now happen. Adam and Eve were exiled from the Garden of Eden and therefore no longer had access to the tree of life. Our first parents would continue to relate, think, plan, manage, and create but not without pain, suffering, and the looming certainty of death and decay.

And so the human race began under these dire terms. Everyone born thereafter has the sinful inclination to be their own god, to decide for themselves what is good and evil. They do not trust nor obey nor rely on nor acknowledge God. God is not in the forefront of their thoughts. They have suppressed any truth about God and who he is. Instead of worshipping the Creator, they worship themselves and the creation. Adam's and Eve's sin in disobeying God resulted into the Fall of mankind, i.e. being born with a sinful nature. We sin because we are sinners; we are not sinners because we sin.

However, in their divine and eternal love for mankind, the Father, the Son, and the Holy Spirit (known as the Holy Trinity, i.e. one in essence, three in person) provided a solution that will restore eternal fellowship with human beings and allow them to once again live in the presence of God. That is, God provided a way to satisfy his judgment against mankind's innate sinful nature to be their own god and make mankind holy and pure again without any trace of sin. This is commonly referred to as God's plan of salvation. This plan would take time to reveal and make it very clear that this plan was indeed from God.

As the human race grew in numbers, God's invisible hand was at work to put his plan of salvation into place. Throughout mankind's history, God began to choose, inspire and had a relationship with certain individuals to carry out certain duties that would give patterns, symbols, and indications as to what God's plan would be. These individuals had faults and failures like us today, but God by his divine grace worked through them to achieve his ultimate purposes.

- Enoch was the seventh generation after Adam. Although not blameless and pure, Enoch nonetheless had a relationship with God. He trusted God for who God was and depended on God to be the one who gave him life. By God's sovereign power, God took Enoch before Enoch experienced death.
- A few generations later, there was a descendant of Enoch named Noah. By God's sovereign plan, Noah was inspired by God to build a huge boat to save his family from God's punishment of mankind for their sinful nature. The punishment was a flood that put to death every human on earth, except Noah's family of eight.
- A few generations later, there was a descendant of Noah named Abraham. Abraham lived circa 2000 BC and was inspired by God to leave his homeland (geographically around southern Iraq) and to settle into a new territory

(geographically around Israel). God promised Abraham that he would start a great nation and would be the father of many nations. Abraham and his wife, Sarah, were ninety and eighty years old respectively. Sarah was well beyond her childbearing years, and therefore, it seemed impossible for her to bear children. Nonetheless, Abraham trusted God to fulfill his promise. Ten years later, they miraculously conceived and had one child, a son named Isaac.

- Later on, God instructed Abraham to sacrifice Isaac in the land of Moriah (the same area where the temple of Israel was later built in Jerusalem circa 1000 BC). Abraham obeyed, believing that God could raise Isaac from the dead, and therefore, still fulfill his promise that Abraham would start a great nation through Isaac. Being pleased with Abraham's obedience, faith, and trust in God, God provided and substituted a ram to be sacrificed instead of Isaac.

- Isaac had twin sons, Esau and Jacob. Before they were born, Jacob the younger was chosen by God to inherit God's blessing and promises to Abraham and to be part of God's unfolding plan of salvation. Jacob had twelve sons, which was the start of the Hebrew nation. God changed Jacob's name to Israel, meaning "struggle with God."

- When Jacob's clan grew, one of Jacob's sons, Joseph, was sold into slavery by his other brothers and ended up in Egypt. About ten years later, the pharaoh made Joseph to be the second most powerful person. Due to a severe famine, Jacob and his clan ended up in Egypt and were taken care of by Joseph. Though Joseph's brothers did evil by selling Joseph into slavery; God meant it for good.

- About 100 years later, the Hebrew nation grew so large, Egypt eventually made them slaves to keep them under control. About another 300 years passed (circa 1500 BC), God chose, inspired, and had a relationship with an individual named Moses (a descendant of Levi, one of Jacob's twelve sons) to follow God's lead and to be his spokesperson. To prove Moses was His spokesperson, God performed signs and wonders through Moses. With God's authority, Moses commanded the pharaoh to let the Hebrew nation leave the land. Pharaoh initially refused. But through many predicted plagues, Pharaoh's heart began to soften as he began to realize God was for real. The last plague was the death of all the firstborn children in the land of Egypt. To avoid this plague from happening in the nation of Israel, Hebrews were to sacrifice a lamb and put the blood on their doorposts. The Angel of Death would see the blood and "pass over" the house without killing the first born. To this day, Passover is celebrated by Hebrews (people of the Jewish faith).

- About a million Hebrews (Israelites) left Egypt and came to the Red Sea. With the pharaoh's army closing in on them, God parted the Red Sea with a strong wind to allow the Hebrew nation to cross and separate them from the Egyptians. Now safe, the nation of Israel ended up spending forty years in the wilderness as they journeyed to the "promised land", i.e. in the same area where Abraham traveled and settled. During the forty years, the Ten Commandments along with other moral commandments and rules of worship and dietary laws were given by God to Moses to be given to the Hebrews. Having these laws distinguished the Israel nation from all the other nations. The people of Israel were known as the "chosen" people; God ultimately created the Israel nation and made a covenant specifically with them.

- Similar to Adam and Eve's situation, God's covenant with the Israel nation was conditional, i.e. if the Israelites kept the Mosaic Law, their life would be blessed including having the blessing of living in the promised land. However, like Adam and Eve who were exiled from Eden, if they disobeyed the commands, they would be exiled from the promised land.

- Of these commandments, there was a sacrificial system as a means to worship God and to remind them of their heritage. There were two particular sacrifices that were performed annually. In the spring, there was the sacrifice of the Passover lamb to remind the Jewish people of their deliverance from the land of Egypt. The other annual sacrifice was the Day of Atonement.

- On the Day of Atonement, one goat was sacrificed as a sin offering. The other goat was used as a symbol to bear all the sins of the Jewish people and was sent out into the wilderness. This is where we get the term "scapegoat." Today the Jewish people celebrate the Day of Atonement on the holiday named Yom Kipper in late September or early October; however, they do not use the two goats.

- The conditional terms of the covenant are part of the Torah, the first five books of what is now commonly referred as the Old Testament. The Old Testament altogether has thirty-nine books written by various authors. Some books are considered historical, e.g. Joshua, Judges, Samuel, Kings, Chronicles, etc. Other books are considered as books of wisdom, e.g. some of the Psalms, Proverbs, etc. The final books are considered prophetic and were written by prophets, e.g. Isaiah, Jeremiah, Ezekiel, Daniel, etc.

- The historic book of Joshua goes into detail of how the Israelites eventually arrived and took over the "promised land,", the same region where Israel is today. The historic book of Judges goes into detail of how certain Jewish leaders ruled and led the nation of Israel for about 500 years after crossing the Red Sea (circa 1500 BC to 1000 BC).

- Circa 1000 BC, there was a descendant of Judah (one of Jacob's twelve sons) named David. David had a close relationship with God and was prophetically told by Samuel (another God-inspired person and the last of the judges) that David would become the king of Israel. When David was king, Nathan (another God-inspired prophet) gave David a word from God: "I will raise up your offspring after you, who shall come from your body, and I will establish his kingdom. He shall build a house for my name, and

I will establish his kingdom forever" (2 Samuel 7:12–13 ESV).

- As a theocratic (God-led) nation, the Israelites as a whole began turning away from their relationship with God. They did not keep up their end of the agreement with God, and thus, the covenant was broken. They eventually were exiled from their land 586/7 B.C.. For a few hundred years between the reign of David to the last king through David's lineage, various prophets as recorded in the prophetic portions of the Old Testament foretold the coming of a Messiah (a Hebrew word that means "the Anointed One") and that the Messiah would restore all things. *This is how the Old Testament ends.*

Within the Old Testament, there are two extremely notable portions of scripture that prophesized a dramatic change that was to take place in the history of mankind.

Behold, the days are coming, declares the Lord, when I will make a new covenant with the house of Israel and the house of Judah, not like the covenant that I made with their fathers on the day when I took them by the hand to bring them out of the land of Egypt, my covenant that they broke, though I was their husband, declares the Lord. But this is the covenant that I will make with the house of Israel after those days, declares the Lord: I will put my law within them, and I will write it on their hearts. And I will be their God, and they shall be my people. And no longer shall each one teach his neighbor and each his brother, saying, "Know the Lord," for they shall all know me, from the least of them to the greatest, declares the Lord. For I will forgive their iniquity and I will remember their sin no more.

(Jeremiah 31: 31–34 ESV, Written in the Old Testament by the prophet Jeremiah circa 600 B.C)

Behold, my servant shall act wisely; he shall be high and lifted up, and shall be exalted. As many were astonished at you—his appearance was so marred, beyond human semblance, and his form beyond that of the children of mankind—so shall he sprinkle many nations; kings shall shut their mouths because of him; for that which has not been told them they see, and that which they have not hear they understand.

Who has believed what they heard from us? And to whom has the arm of the Lord been revealed? For he grew up before him like a young plant, and like a root out of dry ground; he had no form or majesty that we should look at him, and no beauty that we should desire him. He was despised and rejected by men; a man of sorrows, and acquainted with grief; and as one from whom men hide their faces he was despised, and we esteemed him not.

Surely he has borne our griefs and carried our sorrows; yet we esteemed him stricken, smitten by God, and afflicted. But he was wounded for our transgressions; he was crushed for our iniquities; upon him was the chastisement that brought us peace, and with his stripes we are healed. All we like sheep have gone astray; we have turned every one to his own way; and the Lord has laid on him the iniquity of us all.

He was oppressed, and he was afflicted, yet he opened not his mouth; like a lamb that is led to the slaughter, and like a sheep that before its shearers is silent, so he opened not his mouth. By oppression and judgment he was taken away; and as for his generation, who considered that he was cut off out of the land of the living, stricken for the transgressions of my people? And they made his grave with the wicked and with a rich man in his death, although he had done no violence, and there was no deceit in his mouth.

Yet it was the will of the Lord to crush him; he has put him to grief; when his soul makes an offering for sin, he shall see his offspring; he shall prolong his days; the will of the Lord shall prosper in his hand. Out of the anguish of his soul he shall see and be satisfied; by his knowledge shall the righteous one, my servant, make many to be accounted righteous, and he shall bear their iniquities. Therefore I will divide him a portion with the many, and he shall divide the spoil with the strong, because he poured out his soul to death and was numbered with the transgressors; yet he bore the sin of many, and makes intercession for the transgressors. (Isaiah 52: 13 through 53: 12 ESV, Written in the Old Testament by the prophet Isaiah circa 740-701 B.C.)

In the beginning was the Word, and the Word was with God, and the Word was God. He was in the beginning with God. And the Word became flesh and dwelt among us, and we have seen his glory, glory as of the only Son from the Father, full of grace and truth.
—John 1: 1–2,14 ESV, written by the Apostle John

The second half of the Bible, known as the New Testament, has twenty-seven books written by those who lived in the first century, most of whom were eyewitnesses of the Son. The New Testament begins with four Gospels (the word *Gospel* means "Good news") written by Matthew, Mark, Luke and John:

About 1,000 years after King David, there was a descendant of King David named Joseph. Joseph was engaged to Mary. Both Mary and Joseph were visited by an angel named Gabriel (not a fallen angel but a chief angel) to let them know that Mary, who was a virgin, was going to miraculously become pregnant by the power of the Holy Spirit and conceive a child. Out of nothing, something was created by something entirely other—God. Natural science will not be able to explain this supernatural event. This miraculous creation is known as the incarnation of the Son, where the Son took the form of a human body. By doing so, the Son became a second type of Adam. *Gabriel instructed Mary to name this God-man "Jesus," because "He will save his people from their sins"* (Matthew 1:21 ESV).

While on earth and like Adam, the Son was tempted by Satan to break God's commands. Unlike Adam, the Son lived in perfect obedience to the Father. He went on to preach and teach about the

Kingdom of God and having eternal life. He warned about the final judgment when all souls who lived on earth will be either saved from or condemned to spending eternity in hell, a place of darkness, torment and anguish. He further taught about the necessity of being born again (more on this later) and to have an unwavering commitment to fully submit and follow him.

Similar to Moses who performed signs and wonders as an attestation that Moses came in the authority of God, the Son also did signs and wonders that defies natural science. He completely healed anyone who came to him. He multiplied a few fish and a couple loaves of bread to feed thousands of people. He raised people from the dead, walked on water, controlled the weather, and cast out demons. The Son performed supernatural miracles that only something other than this universe could do—God.

The Son proclaimed that he came from heaven and that he was promised Messiah. (The Greek word for Messiah is "Christ". This is why the Son was referred as "Jesus Christ".) He also made it clear that his kingdom is not of this world and that he must suffer first. Among his teachings, the Son made the following astonishing claims about himself.

- "I am the bread of life; whoever comes to me shall not hunger, and whoever believes in me shall never thirst" (John 6:35 ESV).
- "I am the light of the world. Whoever follows me will not walk in darkness, but will have the light of life" (John 8:12 ESV).
- "I am the door. If anyone enters by me, he will be saved and will go in and out and find pasture" (John 10:9 ESV).
- "I am the good shepherd. The good shepherd lays down his life for the sheep" (John 10:11 ESV).
- "I am the resurrection and the life. Whoever believes in me, though he die, yet he will live, and everyone who lives and believes in me shall never die" (John 11:25 ESV).
- "I am the way, the truth, and the life. No one comes to the Father except through me" (John 14:6 ESV).

- "I am the true vine, and my Father is the vinedresser. Every branch of mine that does not bear fruit he takes away, and every branch that does bear fruit he prunes, that it may bear more fruit" (John 15:1–2 ESV).

(The phrase "I am" is the same phrase used by God in the Old Testament when Moses asked God what name he should use for God and God replied, "I AM WHO I AM…I AM has sent me to you". Exodus 3:14 ESV)

Besides making these profound claims, the Son particularly focused on the main reason why he was here on earth. He would be the substitute to take the Father's punishment for man's sin instead of mankind taking the punishment. He would become the sin offering and the scapegoat. He would become the Passover Lamb to spare mankind from death. In fact, the crucifixion happened during the annual Passover celebration. As planned from the time that Adam and Eve disobeyed God's command, the Son descended from the heavenly realm to the earth about 4,000 years later to offer himself as a sacrifice.

On the night before the Son's crucifixion, the Son shared the Passover meal with the Apostles, twelve men whom the Son called to be with him at the beginning of his three-year public ministry. The Son said these words as he broke the bread, "This is my body, which is given for you. Do this in remembrance of me" (Luke 22:19 ESV). After breaking the bread, the Son then took a cup of wine and said, "This cup that is poured out for you is the new covenant in my blood" (Luke 22:20 ESV). This act of breaking bread and drinking from the cup is known as communion and is still conducted today among believers.

That same evening, the Son also told his disciples about how he would be returning to heaven to prepare a place for them and that he would send the Holy Spirit to be with them while they continue their lives on earth. He further explained that, because of their allegiance to him, they too would face persecution but not to be afraid. He has been given by the Father to have full authority over heaven and earth. As prophesied in the Old Testament, the Son will rule as the sovereign King.

By way of crucifixion, the sacrifice of the Son took place on a Friday (which is celebrated today as "Good Friday). The Son rose from the dead three days later on Sunday. The Son still had a human body, but the body was transformed to be an eternal one, i.e. the Son's body would not experience decay and death. Soon after the resurrection, the Son appeared multiple times to the Apostles (minus one named Judas who betrayed the Son to the authorities and later committed suicide in deep regret). The resurrected Son also appeared to others who followed the Son during his three years of earthly ministry. The Son instructed them to wait for the Holy Spirit to descend upon them to give them strength and courage to be a witness of his resurrection and to proclaim who the Son is.

Fifty days later, on the day of Pentecost, the disciples experienced the indwelling of the Holy Spirit and were never the same afterwards. They became bold to proclaim to others about the good news: The Son came to fulfill the writings from the books of Moses and the Prophets, was crucified as God's final sacrifice, and rose again to be the Messiah who rules from heaven forever and ever.

Before the Son ascended into heaven, he foretold to the early followers that he would return again. Unlike his first appearance, which was discreet and from humble beginnings, his return would be in great power and glory. All will see his return, but no one knows when it will happen. It will be a total and shocking surprise. At his second coming, the earth and universe as we know it will end (more on this in a few paragraphs).

Both the Hebrews and the Gentiles (those who were not of Hebrew descent) experienced a radical change within their minds and hearts. This is known as having a "born again" experience. It is a new creation from something other from this universe—God. Because this is a supernatural experience, natural science cannot explain how this happens. As the Son explained, "that which is born of the flesh is flesh, and that which is born of the Spirit is spirit. The wind blows where it wishes, and you hear its sound, but you do not know where it comes from or where it goes. So it is with everyone who is born of the Spirit" (John 3:6,8 ESV).

Being born of the Holy Spirit solely comes from God the Father. No one can buy, earn, or join a church to have this experience. Nor can this experience be inherited from parents. God alone determines if and when this experience happens. To some, it happens early in life. To others, it happens later in life. And to others still, it does not happen at all.

Without this born-again experience, there would be no radical change in mankind's inclinations and desires toward God. Human beings would remain spiritually dead in their sinful state. Like the Son said, "Truly, truly, I say to you, unless one is born again, he cannot see the kingdom of God" (John 3:3 ESV). With this new nature, people have this extra sense. The words from the Son and what is written in the Bible resonates as the truth. The words in the Bible begin to have a profound effect on them.

Born-again individuals have a new innate desire and commitment to turn away from their former rebellious, self-seeking lifestyle and live a new life of obeying and worshipping God. Like Abraham, they too were called by God to have a close relationship with him and to follow him into a new life. They realized that this world is not their home but instead, like Abraham, they were pilgrims who were seeking not a land on earth but a permanent home beyond the grave.

Similar to the nation of Israel that passed through the Red Sea, the early believers were baptized; they completely submerged themselves in water. In a sense, they have been delivered from the bondage of Egypt (sin) and are on their way to the promised land (heaven). They professed publicly that the Son was their Lord and King and pledged their lives to live for him. They recognized that their lives belonged to God, that they were chosen to be adopted and made holy as his children through the price of the Son's sacrifice. They devoted themselves to worship, prayer, studying the scriptures, doing good works of service, and spreading the message of God's plan of salvation. Although their present bodies would continue to struggle against sinful inclinations and experience pain, suffering, decay, and death, they understood that they would someday receive a new eternal body, one like the Son that would be perfect, holy, and without any trace of sin.

The first group of Hebrews and Gentiles eventually called themselves Christians; they associated themselves as servant followers of Christ the Son. Because they were spiritually reborn and made holy by the Son's sacrifice, they became part of his invisible kingdom known as the church. The word "church" in the Greek is translated as "called out ones". Because the Son was raised from the dead on a Sunday, the early Christians would assemble together on Sundays to celebrate and worship, which included taking communion. This is a practice that continues today.

The time between the first appearance and the second appearance of the Son is known as "the last days". During this time there will be a growing intensity of darkness filled with violence, plagues, natural disasters and wars. There will also be an increase of sexual immorality, witchcraft, hatred and other signs of moral decline coupled with prevailing spiritual deception, false teachers and worldly worship of idols. Adding further confusion between the invisible kingdom of light and the earthly kingdom of darkness, Satan disguised himself as an angel of light to infiltrate Christian churches to spread false teaching which leads to false doctrine, false belief, and consequently, divisions within the church.

The ever-travailing world finally ends when the Son, the King of the universe and of his invisible kingdom, returns to bring judgment to every single human being who lived on the face of the earth. The books of their lives will be opened and reviewed. The souls of mankind will be divided into two groups. As the Son described, there will be a separation between sheep and goats, wheat and tares, children of light and children of darkness, children of obedience and children of disobedience.

One group will be those who were born of the Holy Spirt and consequently understood and trusted that the Son was sacrificed and became their scapegoat. During their lives on earth, they were granted by the Father the transaction where all their sins were transferred to the Son, and the Son's spotless perfection was transferred to them. God will declare this group as justified. At the final judgment,

God the Father will see the Son's perfect righteousness in this group of people.

This group of people did not depend on themselves nor anything that they did. They did good works not to be justified but as a response and testimony of God working in their lives. Because the Son made this group holy and pure, they will have eternal incorruptible bodies and go on to live in the presence of God. This group also includes everyone who lived prior to the Son's first appearance and who trusted God for their salvation. Those in the Old Testament times and in the New Testament times shared the same mandate from God: "The righteous shall live by faith" (Habbakuk 2:4 ESV). With the Son's sacrificial atonement for sin, their salvation is now complete.

The other group of people will be those who were not born of the Holy Spirit and therefore had no inclination to repent nor put their trust in the Father's plan of salvation. They did not have any desire to change their ways. The words of the Son and from the Bible had no impact on them. They may have believed in God's existence, but they had no allegiance to God. They depended on themselves and lived for themselves. They did whatever seemed right in their own eyes. They were deceived to think that as long as their good deeds outweigh their bad deeds, they will be good enough to go to heaven, not realizing that without holiness no one will see God. They knew of the Son but never knew the Son. They did not recognize God as their Father nor did the Father recognize them as his adopted children. As the Son stated, "Whoever believes in him is not condemned, but whoever does not believe is condemned already, because he has not believed in the name of the only Son of God. And this is the judgment: the light has come into the world, and people loved the darkness rather than the light because their deeds were evil" (John 3:18–19 ESV).

All the souls in this group will still be blemished and stained with sin. The transfer of the Son's spotless perfection did not happen with them. Instead, they remained unholy and not justified. Without justification and without holiness, there will be a permanent separation from the Father, the Son, and the Holy Spirit. Instead, they will be condemned to eternal damnation, joining Satan and a multitude of demons. They will be forever tormented knowing that they have been permanently exiled to hell, a place of excruciating anguish and darkness, completely separated from those in heaven. Such pain and suffering will continue forever and ever.

As foretold by the prophet Jeremiah 2,600 years ago, what the Father, the Son, and the Holy Spirit accomplished 2,000 years ago is known as the *New Covenant*. The New Covenant is u*nconditional.* As the Apostle Paul wrote to the Christians living in Rome, "From Him, through Him, and to Him are all things. To Him be the glory forever" (Romans 11:36 ESV). Paul further quotes a verse from the Old Testament where God says, "I will have mercy on whom I have mercy, and I will have compassion on whom I have compassion" (Romans 9:15 ESV). As the Son said, receiving eternal life "is impossible with men, but with God all things are possible" (Matthew 19:26 ESV).

People are saved by God alone, by grace alone, and by faith alone. They will be resurrected, and like the Son, they will have new eternal physical bodies to live in God's full presence including all his angels. As Adam and Eve first started, they too will have access to the Tree of Life in a new created world, a new type of Eden, a new promised land. There will be no more death nor decay nor pain nor suffering. There will be no need of the sun, for God himself will be the light. *This concludes a broad summary of what the entire Bible is about.*

Addendum

These are verses found in the Bible that refer to repentance and forgiveness.

> Have mercy on me, O God, according to your steadfast love; according to your abundant mercy blot out my transgressions. Wash me thoroughly from my iniquity, and cleanse me from my sin! The sacrifices of God are a broken spirit; a broken and contrite heart, O God, you will not despise. (Psalms 51:1–2,17 ESV)

> He (the Son) also told this parable to some who trusted in themselves that they were righteous, and treated others with contempt: "Two men went up into the temple to pray, one a Pharisee and the other a tax collector. The Pharisee, standing by himself, prayed thus: 'God, I thank you that I am not like other men: extortioners, unjust, adulterers, or even like this tax collector. I fast twice a week; I give tithes of all I get.' But the tax collector, standing far off, would not even lift up his eyes to heaven, but beat his breast, saying, 'God, be merciful to me, a sinner!' I tell you, this man went down to his house justified, rather than the other. For everyone who exalts himself

will be humbled, but the one who humbles himself will be exalted." (Luke 18:9–14 ESV)

Here is what the Son said regarding becoming a Christian.

And he called to him the crowd with his disciples and said to them, "If anyone would come after me, let him deny himself and take up his cross and follow me. For whoever would save his life will lose it, but whoever loses his life for my sake and the gospel's will save it. For what does it profit a man to gain the whole world and forfeit his life? For what can a man give in return for his life? For whoever is ashamed of me and my words in this adulterous and sinful generation, of him will the Son of Man also be ashamed when he comes in the glory of his Father with the holy angels." (Mark 8:34-38 ESV)[1]

---

[1] A common objection/question regarding Christianity is, "What happens to those who have never heard the Gospel message?" The answer is that none of us deserve God's mercy. If God was obligated to give mercy, then this is not mercy. The fact is that all of us deserve God's judgment and punishment. Therefore, like the penitent tax collector, all of us, no matter where we are on earth, ought to be bowing our heads and pleading for God's mercy. Hearing and knowing the Gospel only makes us more accountable in the final day of judgment.

About the Author

John was raised in a family that did not practice any particular faith. Consequently, he had no understanding of what the Bible was about nor what the Jewish or Christian faith was about. By the time John was in high school, he did not believe that God existed. God was a myth to him.

Between his first and second year of college, John had a powerful spiritual experience. It was like an awakening; he realized that God existed. From that time forth, John was seeing with new eyes. He could look at the stars and know God was out there. He also knew there was some kind of a spiritual world.

Thanks to the help of a book that summarized the Bible, John understood what the Christian faith was about and eventually became one forty years ago. Over the last thirty years, he has read the Bible from cover to cover every year. Over the last twenty years, he has studied theology. Given what he has learned from his own reading and from widely respected theologians throughout church history, John was comfortable to express the Bible's overall message in the form of this summary.

John's hope and prayer is that this summary will help many others understand what is in the Bible and how it all flows as a story from start to finish. The Bible truly is *his* story.

CPSIA information can be obtained
at www.ICGtesting.com
Printed in the USA
JSHW020140260722
28480JS00004B/19